I0799035

THE GHOSTLY TALES OF GRAND RAPIDS

Published by Arcadia Children's Books
A Division of Arcadia Publishing, Inc.
Charleston, SC
www.arcadiapublishing.com

Copyright © 2025 by Julie Rathsack
All rights reserved

Spooky America is a trademark of Arcadia Publishing, Inc.

First published 2025
Manufactured in the United States

Designed by Jessica Nevins
Images used courtesy of Shutterstock.com; p. 38 ehrlif/Shutterstock.com; p. 46 Andrew Jameson/File:LadiesLiteraryClubGrandRapidsMI.jpg Wikimedia Commons/ CC BY-SA 3.0; p. 74 Andrew Jameson/File:AbramWPikeHouseGrandRapidsMI.jpg/ Wikimedia Commons/CC BY-SA 3.0; p. 104 SNEHIT PHOTO/Shutterstock.com.

ISBN: 9781467195980
Library of Congress Control Number: 2025932962

Notice: The information in this book is true and complete to the best of our knowledge. It is offered without guarantee on the part of the author or Arcadia Publishing. The author and Arcadia Publishing disclaim all liability in connection with the use of this book.

All rights reserved. No part of this book may be reproduced or transmitted in any form whatsoever without prior written permission from the publisher except in the case of brief quotations embodied in critical articles and reviews.

Spooky America

The Ghostly Tales of Grand Rapids

Julie Rathsack

Adapted from *A Haunted History of Grand Rapids* by Julie Rathsack

arcadia
CHILDREN'S BOOKS

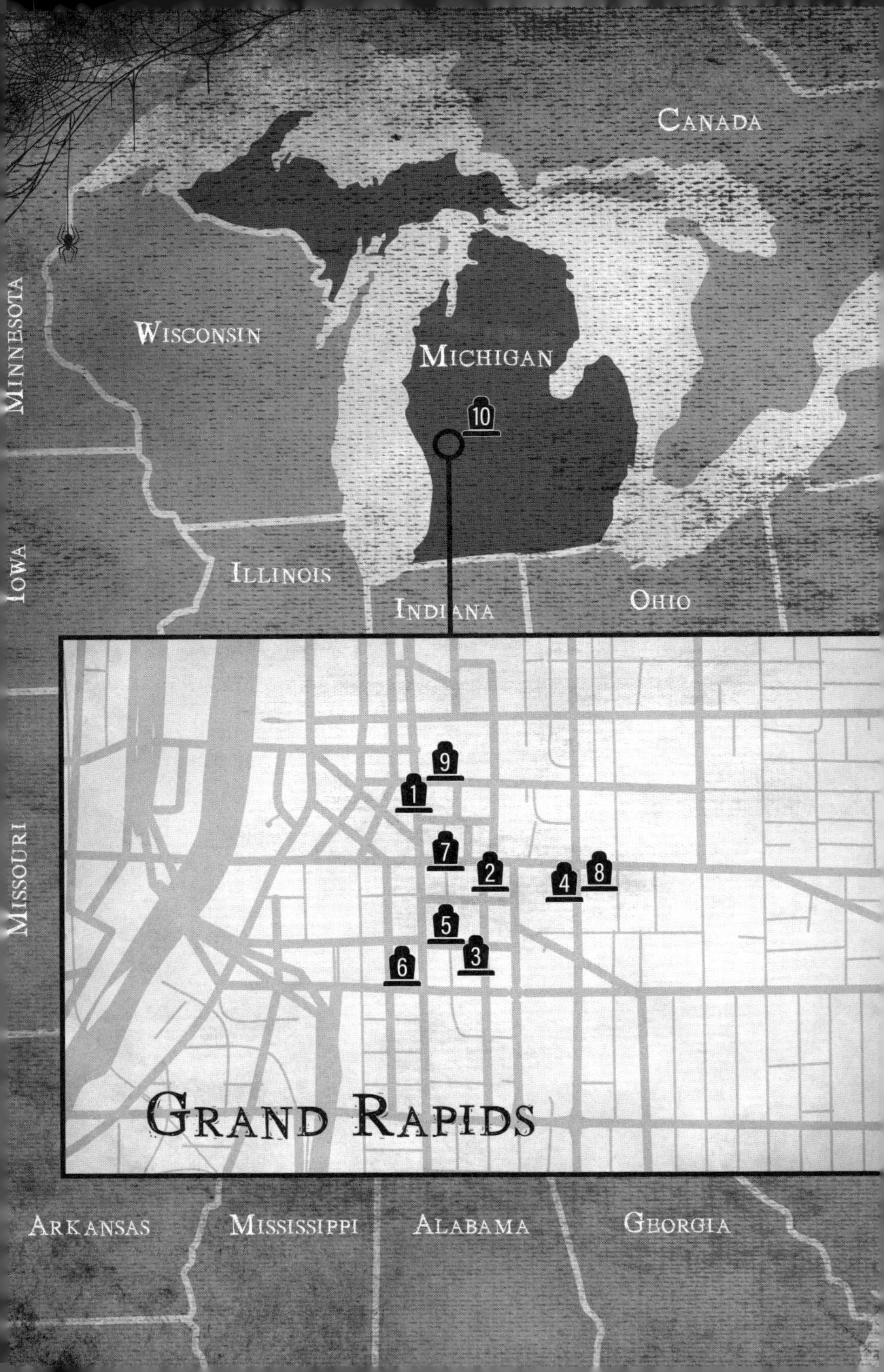
Canada
Minnesota
Wisconsin
Michigan
10
Iowa
Illinois
Indiana
Ohio
Missouri
9
1
7
2
4
8
5
3
6
Grand Rapids
Arkansas
Mississippi
Alabama
Georgia

Table of Contents & Map Key

Welcome to Spooky Grand Rapids!

Have you ever felt a chill run down your spine for no apparent reason? Or sensed an unseen presence watching you? If you live in or have ever visited Grand Rapids, Michigan, there may be a reason for those feelings. Many people know that Grand Rapids is reputed to be haunted, but few realize that stories of ghostly encounters, disappearances, and other mysterious phenomena have surrounded the city long before its official founding in 1850.

In the early 18th century, Indigenous peoples referred to the area now known as Grand Rapids as "the Haunted Valley of the Grand." They believed that malevolent spirits roamed the land. It wasn't unusual for individuals or even entire hunting parties to vanish in the forests along the Grand River, never to be seen or heard from again. These tales of ghostly apparitions continued to be told around campfires for generations.

I was born and raised in Grand Rapids, in what some might call a "haunted house." From the outside, it appeared to be a typical home. On the inside, however, it was anything but ordinary. Objects moved on their own, strange shadows walked down our hallway, and unexplained voices were heard day and night. It scared the living daylights out of me when anything happened! But after the terrifying moments passed, I found myself curious as to why it was happening. I began to collect and learn anything I could about hauntings and ghosts, but none of it answered my question of who they were and why they were there.

One night, when I was fourteen, my cousin Jennifer stayed overnight. We thought it would be fun to use a Ouija board (which I don't recommend!). We set up my bedroom with candles, casting flickering shadows on the walls. The room was dim and filled with an eerie silence, broken only by the occasional hum of passing cars outside. We asked the board if anyone was there. The planchette moved to "YES." We asked for a name, and it spelled out "FORTUNA." The room started to feel super creepy, like the air was thick with something unseen. We freaked out and put the board away. Later, we laughed about how the ghost might be doing things "for tuna."

Over a year later, my mom was cleaning out the front closet and found an old church directory. She said, "This is from before we lived here. I wonder if the previous owners went to our church?" I flipped through the pages and almost jumped out of my skin when I saw our address listed under an elderly couple, the Fortunas, smiling brightly at me in the picture. It felt like a lightning bolt had hit me. The answers I was

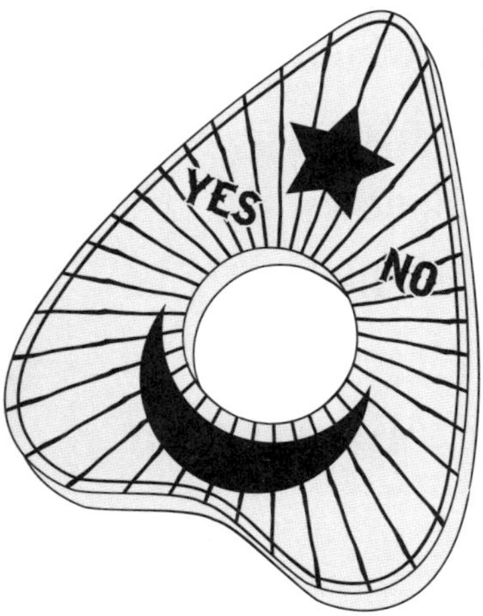

looking for weren't in ghost books; they were in the past!

That's how I became a historian. I spent countless hours in local libraries and city archives researching haunted places. I discovered that most local hauntings have some twisted history behind them. My fascination grew so much that I began writing books about these eerie tales and started conducting ghost tours downtown called "Ghosts of Grand Rapids." Over a decade later, I'm still going strong, despite competition from other tour companies who read my books and retell my stories. If you're looking for the original and most authentic ghost tours, look for me!

What I found is that Grand Rapids has a rich past, earning the nickname "Furniture City" due to its many furniture factories. Heritage

Hill, the oldest neighborhood in Grand Rapids, boasts over 1,300 homes dating back to 1843 and is on the National Register of Historic Places. It is also the birthplace of Gerald R. Ford, the 38th President of the United States.

This city is full of wonders for people to enjoy. You can explore art, plants, and butterflies from around the world at Frederik Meijer Gardens & Sculpture Park. John Ball Zoo is a fun place to learn about animals and conservation. The Grand Rapids Public Museum showcases fascinating exhibits, including the Streets of Old Grand Rapids. The city also hosts exciting events like ArtPrize, LaughFest, and Grand Rapids Comic Con throughout the year. Although the dense forests have given way to concrete, bricks, and glass, many believe that the spirits encountered by the area's Indigenous peoples still haunt this land, causing disturbances among the living. Those places you are going to have a past!

Is Grand Rapids haunted? Many people think so. As you read the following stories, you can decide for yourself.

CHAPTER 1

The Ghost of Dr. Alfred

On the corner of Fountain Street and Ionia Avenue, you will see a four-story brick building with rows of windows. While it looks like a typical office from the outside, this structure has stood for over a century, and if you listen closely, you might hear whispers of its haunted past.

Many years ago, a kind and hardworking man named Dr. Alfred Webster worked in the building for the New Era Association Insurance

Company. He was known for being a good neighbor who loved helping people. Dr. Alfred had been married three times, through no fault of his own. His first wife passed away when their son was a little boy. His second wife also died young, leaving him with two daughters. Finally, he married another woman named Hattie, who was much younger than him. In fact, she was three years younger than Alfred's youngest child!

Despite having so many setbacks in life, Dr. Alfred did all he could to support his family. He even helped his son-in-law, Charles, married to his oldest daughter, Ida, get a job at his office. But even with all he did for others, he may have been hiding a secret that would change how people thought of him.

You see, a large sum of money had gone missing from the company where Dr. Alfred worked. The amount was $14,594, which is like

$500,000 today. Coincidentally, Dr. Alfred was building a new house on Reed's Lake that cost the exact same amount. Some people began to wonder if Dr. Alfred had taken the money to pay for his new home.

On a chilly autumn day, September 30, 1909, Dr. Alfred was discovered by his son-in-law in his office, lying on the couch, covered in blood. It appeared that the doctor had meticulously removed his coat and vest, unbuttoned his shirt, and shot himself through the heart. Beside him lay a note explaining that he had tried to do good but couldn't fight against the powerful people opposing him. He believed he had given honest service and earned everything he received from New Era, but if there was anything still owed, he paid it with his life.

As news of his death spread through town, people were shocked. Dr. Alfred was known for his cheerful demeanor and constant smile. How could this happen? It was revealed that the night before his death, Dr. Alfred had become violently ill at home, prompting his family to call doctors. Rumors began to circulate that he had taken morphine in an attempt to end his life, but his family had found him before it was too late. Tragically, the very next day, Dr. Alfred seemed to have found another way, using a gun to end his life instead.

To many people in Grand Rapids, however, the details didn't add up. Whispers began to circulate that there was something more sinister at play, particularly involving the son-in-law. Was it a coincidence that Charles had found Dr. Alfred's body? And what about the fact that he took over Dr. Alfred's job as soon as the doctor was out of the way? If neither of those points seemed suspicious, consider that Charles soon divorced Dr. Alfred's daughter and married his widow, Hattie. Before long, friends and neighbors started to wonder: Had Dr. Alfred intentionally ended his life, or had he been murdered? There was much speculation, but nothing was ever proven.

As for the beautiful house by the lake, it was sold to a new owner, Mr. Mills. He had planned to raise frogs there, as "frog leg dinners" were all the rage at the local restaurants. That plan never came together for him, and he eventually rented out the property. Over the years, the house fell into disrepair and was eventually torn down. Today, all that remains are the stone columns at the entrance, standing like silent sentinels outside of Waterfront Park in East Grand Rapids.

But the story doesn't end there. The building where Dr. Alfred died became known for strange occurrences. People have reported seeing ghostly figures, hearing unexplained noises, and feeling a chill in the air. One night, a woman named Rosa, who worked as a cleaner, had a terrifying encounter.

Rosa was cleaning the third floor of the building when she realized she had forgotten her broom. She took the elevator down to the second floor, where the lights flickered ominously. As she walked down the hallway, she felt like someone was watching her. But when she entered the office to get her broom, the light turned on by itself.

Suddenly, Rosa saw an older gentleman standing in front of her, dressed in old-fashioned clothes. She screamed and dropped the broom. "I'm sorry! I didn't realize someone was still working!" she apologized. The man continued to silently stare at her and then vanished. Rosa was terrified and hurried back to the elevator. As the doors closed, Rosa looked up and saw the man quickly walking toward her down the long dark hallway. He looked pale and gaunt, with dark circles under his eyes and blood trickling from his mouth. The doors shut just as he was about to reach her.

Rosa never saw the ghost again, but others in the building reported similar experiences. Doors would slam shut on their own, lights would flicker, and sometimes, people heard the sound of a gunshot echoing through the halls.

Years later, a picture of Dr. Alfred was shown to Rosa, and she immediately recognized him as the ghost she had seen. She shivered with fear, remembering his sad eyes.

To this day, people say that Dr. Alfred's spirit still haunts the building, watching over those who enter. Some believe he is trying to clear his name, while others think he is searching for peace. If you ever visit 82 Ionia Avenue, be sure to look out for the ghost of Dr. Alfred. You might catch a glimpse of him, standing silently in the shadows, waiting to tell his story.

CHAPTER 2

The Bloody Man

Do you believe in bad luck? Frank Hibben Stout certainly had his share of it. His dad died before he was even born, his sister was blind, and his mother struggled to support the family. Out of desperation, Frank's mom put him up for adoption at an orphanage. Frank was taken in by a farmer who needed help on his land. The only good thing that came out of it was Ada, Frank's new foster sister. Although she was two years younger, they quickly became best friends. Wherever Ada went, Frank went, and vice versa. As they got older, and Ada's parents pushed her to get married, Frank got jealous. He didn't want Ada to give attention to anyone but him. Still, Ada married and moved away. Soon after, Frank met a lady, and they had a little girl. Three years later, the baby caught scarlet fever and died. Eventually, Frank and his former love broke up.

In 1908, Frank met and married a woman named Marie. They moved to Grand Rapids and bought a house on Adams Street. Frank found a job at the Stile's Brothers Lumber Company, but he still wasn't happy. He always thought about Ada. He had been so angry after she started a new life with her husband that he never even spoke her name. In fact, his wife Marie didn't even know Ada existed. Frank began to drink heavily, and he and Marie constantly fought about money. He spent so much of his paychecks on alcohol that they were close to losing their home.

Imagine Frank's excitement when, walking downtown one day, he looked up to see Ada smiling at him. She was just as surprised to see him, a familiar face in a strange city! Unfortunately, she and her husband had divorced, leaving Ada to take a housekeeping job for Dr. Groner on Sheldon Avenue. They went to lunch and reminisced about old times. Frank told Ada how unhappy he was and asked to borrow $600 to save his house. That was a lot of money in those days, but Ada wanted to help. She gave him the money, and they went on their way.

When word got back to Marie that Frank had been seen about town with another woman, she immediately kicked him out of the house and filed for divorce. Frank rented an upstairs room at the Fulton, a historic twenty-six-room boardinghouse built by the Buchanan family, prominent figures in Grand Rapids history.

Frank was ready for a new start. He knew his wife was done with him, so he decided to move to Detroit, hoping for better opportunities. He told Ada about his plan. At first, she thought it was a good idea and hoped it would help him get his life together. But then Frank had another idea: he wanted Ada to come with him and be his housekeeper. Ada wasn't interested.

"Frank, I have a life here in Grand Rapids. I'm not leaving," she said. Frank got really angry. He grabbed Ada by the neck, but she fought back and managed to escape. She ran back to her boardinghouse and told everyone, "Frank has gone crazy and wants to kill me!"

The next day, Frank came to apologize, but

Ada refused to see him. He called and begged, saying he was leaving the next day, but she still refused. Two days passed, and there was no sign of Frank. Everyone thought he had left for Detroit, but Ada was still careful. Before going to work on Friday, she wrote a note saying, "If anything happens to me, please tell my sister," and left it on her nightstand. She also told a friend, "If Frank finds me today, he will kill me."

On Friday, December 10, 1915, Ada walked to work as usual. She arrived at Dr. Groner's house and started her chores. Everything seemed fine until she saw Frank peeking through the window. She quickly checked the doors; they were locked. Ada stood in the hallway, unsure what to do. Then she heard someone at the door. She was relieved to see it was just the other housekeeper. But before she could close the door, Frank pushed his way in. Ada's heart sank.

At that moment, Dr. Groner came home and asked Frank to leave. Frank left, but Ada was still scared. Later, as she walked down Fulton Street, Frank appeared and grabbed her arm. He forced her to walk to his rooming house. In front of the building, Ada tried to escape. She ran inside, crying for help. She burst into a room where two women were having tea.

"Save me! Save me!" she screamed. Frank followed her in and shouted, "I've got you, Ada!" He pulled out a gun and shot her twice. Ada fell to the floor, and the women screamed in fear. Frank didn't seem to notice them. He walked upstairs to his room, looked in the mirror, and shot himself. Ada was taken to the hospital, but it was too late. She died from

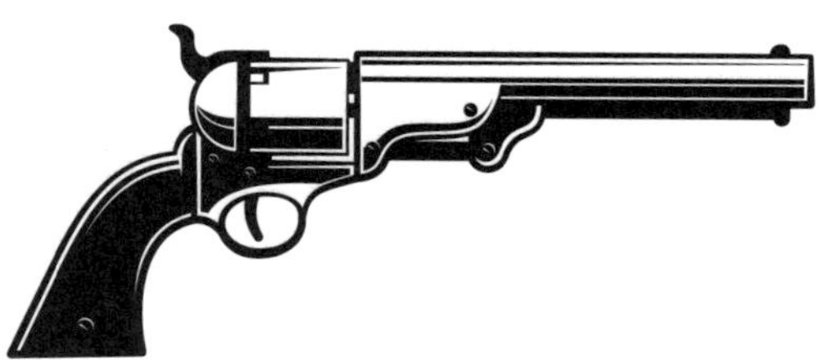

her injuries. Not long after the deaths, the home was torn down, and in its place, a small, one-story building was built of brick.

Over the years, many businesses have come and gone in this building, from medical equipment to college textbooks. In the 1990s, a woman named Beth spoke about something terrifying she saw in the basement.

Beth was carrying boxes down to storage when she saw what appeared to be a man standing at the bottom of the steps. Dripping in what appeared to be blood, she instantly noticed something even more upsetting.

"He had no pupils! He was sopping wet in what looked like dark red blood... and all I could see were the whites of his eyes!" Beth threw the boxes at him, grabbed her keys, and ran out the door. She refused to work alone after that.

More recently, the building became a popular restaurant called MeXo Tequila & Mezcal Bar. The executive chef, Oscar Moreno, is famous for adding a modern twist to traditional Mexican dishes. The restaurant was even named "Restaurant of the Year" by *Grand Rapids Magazine* in 2024.

The employees whisper that everyone who works there knows the place is haunted, especially the basement. The spirit of a man has been seen lurking near a room they refer to as the chemical room.

"We all feel completely creeped out down there," one employee said, "and at least four people have seen him vanish right before their eyes."

The bartender, who didn't believe in ghosts when he started working at MeXo, does now after witnessing bottles and glasses moving around on the bar by themselves. One time, a glass mysteriously exploded when no one was near it.

The next time you are driving past the small white building on Fulton Street, think of Frank. He made some good choices and some bad ones, but each decision shaped his journey. Remember, it's not all about the luck you have, but what you do with it. When life gets tough, face it bravely and make choices that lead to a brighter future. You have the power to create your own luck! And if you go inside for some of that amazing Mexican food, you might bump into Frank to tell him yourself!

CHAPTER 3

The Screaming Woman of Hotel Browning

Downtown on Sheldon Boulevard, there stands a large building that has been transformed into studio apartments. Only one small clue remains of its incredible history—the words "Hotel Browning" etched into the cement above the entryway.

The hotel's story began with a tragic event. A mason named Thomas Burns had a terrible accident while standing on top of the partially built structure. Curiosity got the best of him when he looked down to see the freshly poured cement. He lost his balance and fell to the ground, striking a beam on his way down. He died soon after, the first of many to meet an unfortunate end on the property.

When the Hotel Browning opened in 1917, it was a magnificent six-floor building with a bowling alley, billiards, and the best café in town. It was the place to be! Famous guests like Babe Ruth and Spencer Tracy had stayed there, impressed by the hotel's luxurious rooms, each with its own bathroom (which wasn't common at the time).

It was a bright and sunny day on July 2, 1917, when Mr. James Wilmer Hunter and his wife, Emma, left their old house for the last time. They

had sold it and were moving into their new apartment in the Hotel Browning. Both were excited for the new adventure! James and the hotel staff carried their belongings up to their new flat on the fourth floor, while Emma started unpacking.

As the day turned into evening, James went downstairs to thank the staff for their hard work with a tip. After, he stepped into the elevator with Mrs. J. B. Mooney (who lived on the third floor) and the elevator operator. Unlike modern elevators, which have automatic doors and floor buttons, elevators in those days were manually operated by a person using a controller. They lacked many of the safety measures we take for granted today.

"Fourth floor, please," James said with a smile. But as the elevator stopped on the third floor, Mrs. Mooney stepped out. James was still fidgeting with his wallet and, thinking it was his floor, tried to follow. Suddenly, the elevator shot upward, and James was caught in the doorway. His head was crushed, and he died instantly. Trying to help the situation, the elevator operator reversed the controls causing the body to dangle in the elevator shaft where James was hit a second time, almost cutting his body in half.

Emma was heartbroken. The hotel staff walked her down the steps to the main sitting area where she sobbed and wailed for hours. Instead of a happy new beginning, she was left alone in a place filled with sorrow. She moved back to her old home, unable to bear the memories of that tragic day.

As years passed, the Hotel Browning began to fall into disrepair. Newer hotels started popping up, so the owners began to rent the space to different businesses. One of them was a place called the Neal Institute. This place claimed it could help people cure their drug and alcohol problems in just three days, which was dishonest and misleading. Sometimes, the Neal Institute got in trouble because they didn't take good care of their patients.

Eventually, the building was sold to the Ferguson Hospital. It was about that time that strange things began to happen. People reported seeing a woman wandering the halls and crying out in pain. Some believed it was Emma Hunter, mourning her lost husband. Others thought it might be one of the many patients who had died.

One of the most chilling stories came from Chris, a former employee of the Ferguson Hospital. She had worked there for over four years and had several eerie encounters with the ghostly woman in gray.

One day, Chris was preparing examination rooms when she heard a woman cry out in terror. She quickly investigated the hallway and saw a nurse standing against the wall, covering her face with her hands. Chris walked up to comfort her, but as she put her hand on the woman's shoulder, the nurse jumped a mile high. Once she uncovered her eyes and saw Chris, she hugged her tight and would not let go. Chris asked the nurse what was wrong, but she was so scared she couldn't even talk.

Chris looked around for anything out of the ordinary that could have upset her coworker. The nurse pointed at two closed doors at the end of the hall. Suddenly, Chris heard the exact same scream come from the end of the hallway and watched as the upper half of a woman floated through the door on the right.

The ghostly woman had her hair loosely pulled back into a bun. Messy strands of hair were matted on her tearstained cheeks, and dark circles sat under her black eyes. With the bright hallway lights, Chris could make out veins showing through the ghostly entity's paper-thin skin. She could only see the upper half of the woman's body, all of which appeared to be gray.

The specter seemed to pause for a moment

as she looked directly into the eyes of the two women standing before her. Slowly, her lips curled back into a wicked smile that exposed rotting teeth between her thin lips. Suddenly, the wraith let out another wretched wail and disappeared into thin air.

Chris and the nurse were shaken up and could not understand what they had seen. As time passed, they began to joke about what they saw as their "little secret." While there were always rumors about the building being haunted, no one ever talked about it because they didn't want to look crazy, especially in a professional environment. Chris heard the wailing a few more times but never saw the terrifying spirit again, for which she added, "Thank God!"

The ghost of Hotel Browning remains a mystery. Is it Emma Hunter weeping in despair for the husband she lost so suddenly? Or is it one of the patients who walked in through the doors of a hospital, only to be carried out in a body bag? We may never know.

Amway Grand Plaza Hotel

CHAPTER 4

The Sweet Spot

Martin Sweet was born in 1819 in the small town of Paris, New York. As a young boy, he worked in his family's flour mill and attended school like any other kid. Unfortunately, at the age of fourteen, his father passed away, and Martin became the man of the family. He decided to save his money, which proved to be a smart move.

At twenty-three, Martin moved to Michigan and worked hard, eventually becoming the head of several companies. In Delhi, he built his own flour mill with the money he had been saving. In 1844, Martin married Submit Desdemona Higgins, the daughter of a New York lumber baron known for her great beauty. Desdemona, as she preferred to be called, disliked her first name. Together, they moved to Grand Rapids in 1846 and started their family.

Over the following years, Martin embarked on many different ventures, excelling in everything from mills to furniture and cattle. He brought the first Holstein-Friesian cattle to Michigan and raised them on his farm, which was located where Sweet Street Park now stands. He built the first grain elevator in town by the railroad, making it easy to load and unload the box cars. Martin also established the first real bank in Grand Rapids.

In 1860, Martin was persuaded to run for mayor on the Republican ticket. Despite Grand Rapids being a predominantly Democratic town, he won by a landslide because everyone admired his work ethic and generous spirit.

At the time, Fulton Street was home to the most prominent members of society, and Martin wanted to be part of it. He and Desdemona purchased two lots on the southwest corner of Fulton Street and Lafayette Avenue and built a magnificent home, completed around 1863, which still stands today.

In 1868, Martin decided to leave the milling business and build an impressive hotel by the Grand River. He named it the Sweet's Hotel. However, he soon realized there was a problem: the hotel was built on a corner with a sharp turn and a four-foot drop in the street level. The dirt roads made it difficult for horse-drawn wagons to navigate, and the lower ground next to the river flooded every spring. To solve this, Martin decided to raise the building four feet. He lined up men with 1,800 screw jacks under the building, and at the signal of a whistle, the workers would turn the jacks simultaneously, raising the building evenly, a quarter of an inch with each turn. By the end, everyone was exhausted, but Martin's building had been successfully lifted!

In 1902, Martin sold the hotel to James Boyd Pantlind, and it was renamed the Pantlind Hotel. This hotel had every luxury imaginable at the time, including phones in every room. It even held the architectural title for the largest gold-leafed ceiling in the world in its lobby. In 1978, Amway Corporation purchased this historic landmark, restoring the Pantlind to its original 1920s design and adding restaurants, shops, and large

meeting and banquet halls. Over 150 years later, this hotel is still known as one of the finest in America.

With so many people coming and going, the hotel has seen lots of tragedy. In 1899, Amelia Rice, the wife of the hotel's manager, died of cancer in her living quarters on the upper floor. She left behind her loving husband and two children. In 1906, a man named Hiram Mills had a heart attack in the restaurant. Another guy, Charles Purcell, had a massive stroke in the café in 1912.

The most unfortunate death happened in 1914. A maid named Mary Monko finished working for the day. Back then, the cleaning staff were offered sleeping quarters on the upper floor of the hotel. Mary got on the elevator with her friend and co-worker, Josephine Kreuko. Happy to be done with work, the two girls were acting silly. As Mary stepped off the elevator, Josephine playfully grabbed the controls from the operator's hands. The elevator jerked downward, and Mary's head was caught between an iron gate and the tenth-floor landing. She was decapitated instantly. Though she died, her spirit seems to have lived on.

In the old days, smoking inside was normal, but a mischievous spirit didn't approve of it in the old section of the hotel. If a guest left behind a dirty ashtray, it would disappear. If someone set their cigarettes down, the pack would also disappear. Perhaps Mary was just cleaning up. This is the same area where the apparition of a maid has been seen.

The ghost of a young boy has been spotted wandering the hallways, often following people as they walk, only to vanish when they notice him. He has been seen several times when the elevator doors open, standing with his hands folded behind his back before disappearing. Could he be one of Amelia Rice's children, searching for his mother?

Many visitors who stay in the older section of the hotel have had strange experiences. Blankets are tugged off beds, belongings get moved around, and people often feel hands tucking them in as they fall asleep. One gentleman was woken up during the night by two men loudly conversing outside his room. When he opened the door to ask them to keep it down, he found nothing except an icy chill.

Could the spirit of Mary Monko still be cleaning up after guests? Or is it another ghostly presence making itself known? Despite its eerie tales, the Amway Grand Plaza Hotel's unique blend of history and modern amenities make it a beloved destination for both the curious and the comfort-seeking traveler.

Ladies' Literary Club

CHAPTER 5

Clara's Staircase

In the late 1800s, during a time called the Gilded Age, many people believed that women should stay at home. But some women wanted to learn new things and educate themselves. This is how the Ladies' Literary Club on Sheldon Boulevard began.

Marion Louise Withey was one of the first women to start a club to educate women in Grand Rapids. She was born in Vermont in

1829 and moved to Grand Rapids (which was called the village of Kent back then) when she was six years old. She grew up and married a judge named Solomon Lewis Withey, who was appointed by President Abraham Lincoln. During the Civil War, Marion worked hard to get supplies for hospitals and the Union army. She helped start a school called the Union Benevolent Association (UBA) Training School for Nurses. She was also involved in starting Park Congregational Church, which began as a prayer service in her father's home. She was a very busy woman!

By 1870, many women joined the club, and they formed the Ladies' Literary Association. Marion became president in 1871 and helped start the very first public library in town. In 1882, the group officially became the Ladies' Literary Club of Grand Rapids.

The club grew so much that they needed

a new building. They found a lot on Sheldon Boulevard and hired an architect named William G. Robinson to design it. The building had a slate roof and beautiful stained-glass windows, including one made by Tiffany, a famous glass designer, in 1915.

Over the years, the Ladies' Literary Club hosted famous guests like U.S. presidents Theodore Roosevelt, William Howard Taft, and Woodrow Wilson. They also rented out the building for concerts and plays. In 1971, it was added to the National Register of Historic Places.

Marion Withey passed away in 1912 from a blood clot in her brain, but her legacy lived on. The club continued to thrive until 2005, when it eventually disbanded. Since then, it has been used as an event space for weddings, shows, and more.

Most people who pass by the building don't realize it holds a secret. For over one hundred years, a woman has been seen crying on the stairs. There has been a lot of speculation about who the sad lady is. Some believe it is Marion Withey, weeping for her old life. But having accomplished so much while alive, this seems unlikely. Another woman seems to fit the bill a little better; her name was Clara Greene.

Clara was born in 1848 in New York and raised by her mother, Sophia. The two were extremely close. When Clara was twenty-five, they moved to Grand Rapids where Clara had been hired as a schoolteacher. She joined the Ladies' Literary Club and was happy to share her vast knowledge with the other members. Everything was going great until her mother died suddenly in 1885. Clara was absolutely devastated! She quit her teaching job and started to spend all her time at the Ladies' Literary Club. She held many different roles, including corresponding secretary and chairman, and she gave lots of presentations. She tried to forget about her mom by keeping herself busy, and it worked . . . for a little while.

On a scorching July day in 1903, Clara set out for a walk and never returned. The last person to see her noted that, despite the sweltering heat in the nineties, Clara was dressed in a black wool skirt, a white linen shirt, and a black hat. She stopped by a neighbor's farmhouse to borrow a small pail of water, and from there, she vanished.

Her friends looked everywhere, even

placing ads in the newspaper, hoping someone had seen Clara. Nine days later, two women walking through the woods near Walker Avenue stumbled upon a body. It was badly decomposed due to the heat and insects, and they couldn't tell who it was. The only clue they had was the body's clothing: the very *same* clothing Clara had on when she was last seen. Beside the body, Clara's friends found small white papers and an empty cup. The autopsy revealed that Clara had intentionally ingested strychnine, a poison, to end her life.

Over the years, people have seen the woman's ghost many times, but she never talks to anyone. Her spirit is what paranormal researchers call a "residual haunting." This means that strong feelings, like sadness, can leave a kind of energy behind in a place. That energy can show up as sights, sounds, or even smells, like a replay of the past. Unlike other ghosts that might try to talk to people, a residual haunting is more like a recording that plays over and over without noticing anyone around. Most people in the field don't even believe that the woman's spirit is stuck in the building. It's just an imprint on the environment.

One volunteer named Tyler had an experience when he was one of only a handful of people in the building. He was setting up the auditorium for an event, when he heard weeping coming from the front foyer. He followed the sound and noticed the air became colder and colder as he got closer. Sitting halfway up the steps, her head buried in her hands, was a sobbing woman. Though she seemed solid, Tyler could tell by her clothes that she was not from this time. Feeling her immense sadness, Tyler looked up at her and asked, "Are you okay?"

The woman didn't respond. Tyler sat there and watched her weep for what felt like minutes but was probably more like seconds. Finally, she picked her head up. Her cheeks were stained by tears, and her big eyes appeared to look up toward the heavens as she vanished right in front of him. Later that night, after Tyler shared what he'd experienced, someone showed him a picture of Marion Withey. Right away, Tyler verified that it was not the same woman he had seen. To this day, he has never seen a picture of Clara Greene.

Clara spent much of her time at the Ladies' Literary Club, both before and after her mother Sophia's passing. She likely created many wonderful memories there over the years. Unfortunately, the deep sorrow she felt from losing her mom seems to have left a mark on the place. Yet, despite this sadness, there's a bright side. The clubhouse is known for hosting fantastic events, creating new and joyful memories for everyone who visits. Weddings, anniversaries, and parties regularly fill the place with happiness. These positive energies are gradually replacing the old, sad memories, bringing a fresh, uplifting atmosphere to the club every day. May both these remarkable women rest in peace, as they deserve, for they did so much to help others during their lives.

CHAPTER 6

Coliseum of the Dead

Do you ever wonder where people went for big events before the Van Andel Arena was built? Well, on Commerce Street, there's a huge brick building that used to be known as the Coliseum. Its entrance has a large archway, decorated with carved lion heads on each side. It was built by a man named Henry Heystek, who came to America from the Netherlands when he was a boy.

Henry's parents taught him that to be successful, he had to learn more and learn it fast! He quickly picked up English and completed all eight grades of elementary school in just two years. At fifteen, he faced a heartbreaking loss when both his parents died. But he continued to work hard and save his money, eventually opening a successful paint and wallpaper business.

By the time Henry turned twenty-two, he had saved $900 and had the brilliant idea of building a roller-skating rink that could also be used for big meetings and parties. The Coliseum opened in 1910 and quickly became a popular place to hang out. It could hold up to eight hundred skaters, and Henry would bring in an eight-piece orchestra for music. He even hired famous performers like Harley Davidson, a roller-skating and ice-skating champion. Since there was no television or Internet in those days, everyone looked at the Coliseum for entertainment.

Another famous friend who visited frequently was Alice Teddy, a roller-skating bear! She was a 215-pound cinnamon bear, adopted by a man named George B. Crapsey after her mother died when she was four months old. George found that when he put on his roller skates around Alice, she would try to imitate him. One day, for a laugh, he fitted her up with skates and off she went! Alice Teddy traveled the country in a little skirt, racing in roller derbies, shaking hands, and giving hugs. Henry had a sellout crowd every time she appeared in town.

On January 22, 1912, the *Evening Press* wrote an article called "Not Very Serious." It said that Henry was sick at home with an upset stomach, but that he would be fine. Everyone was shocked when, the very next day, the newspaper announced that Henry Heystek had died from pneumonia. He was only fifty years old at the time of his death. Before dying, he had changed his will, donating big amounts of cash to charitable places around the city, like hospitals, orphanages, and the Salvation Army.

So, is the Coliseum haunted by the spirit of a roller-skating bear? As amazing as that would be, that is not who our Coliseum ghost is. Instead, it is believed to be a man who lived across the street and whose life was filled with tragedy.

Charles Santman was born in a small town in Ohio. When he was seventeen, he was playing around on train tracks with friends, which is never a good idea. He ended up getting hit by a train and doctors had to insert a silver plate into his head where his skull

had been crushed. Charles recovered, and in 1907, he moved to Grand Rapids with his wife, Mary. He started a business hauling ashes for neighbors, and life seemed great until 1914.

That year, all four of his children got measles. A month after that, his youngest son got pneumonia and died two days after his first birthday. Charles was heartbroken and started to drink a lot of alcohol. One month later, their three-year-old son unexpectedly died of typhoid. Before he was even buried, their eight-year-old daughter caught it and was taken to St. Mary's Hospital.

That night, after returning to their apartment, Charles and Mary were both exhausted. The past couple of months had been a nightmare. As they looked around their quiet apartment, Charles said, "There are too many bad memories here. We should move and start somewhere fresh." He told his wife to start packing and that he would find some boxes to put their things in, as he walked out the door.

The following morning, Mary woke to find that Charles had never come home. She assumed he had passed out somewhere or was still out drinking. It wasn't until a policeman knocked on the door that she knew something was wrong. They had found Charles's body in the alley behind the Coliseum. In addition to lots of alcohol, he drank an entire bottle of poisonous chloroform to end his life.

Soon after, strange things began happening around the Coliseum. People reported seeing a man in a brown derby hat, exactly like the one Charles used to wear. Today, the Coliseum has different businesses on the ground floor with apartments upstairs. Sightings of a restless spirit continue to be seen. Lights turn on and off by themselves, and objects move, particularly toward the rear of the building that lines the old alley.

A woman named Jennifer lived in an apartment on the second floor of the Coliseum. One chilly evening, she had plans with her boyfriend Dean to go to a show at the Van Andel Arena. Jennifer had to work late, so Dean decided to surprise her with a homemade meal. He got the key and went into her apartment alone.

As he turned on the burner, the flame flickered and danced wildly, as if someone playful was blowing on it. Curious and a bit uneasy, Dean leaned closer to the stove. In the reflection of the big silver stock pot filled with boiling water, he saw the shadowy figure of a man leaning down right next to him, wearing a brown derby hat. Dean's heart pounded in his chest!

Terrified, he bolted out of the apartment

and waited for Jennifer outside. When she finally arrived, he breathlessly told her about the ghostly figure he had seen. Jennifer laughed at first, but when Dean described the man, her face turned pale. She became quiet, and it took Dean all night to get her to explain why she was so upset.

Finally, with a trembling voice, Jennifer confessed that ever since she had moved into the apartment, she had been having nightmares. In them, a man in a brown derby hat would stand over her bed, whispering the same chilling words, "Is it you?" before vanishing into thin air.

Who could this ghostly figure be? Is it Henry Heystek checking on his beloved Coliseum? Or is it Charles

Santman looking for his wife to apologize for leaving her the way he did. The true identity of the ghost remains a mystery, but his presence adds to the spooky charm of the old Coliseum. His spirit continues to linger in the halls of the old building, adding to its mystique and making it a place where history and the supernatural intertwine.

CHAPTER 7

Mortimer's Mysterious Adventures

It was still dark outside when fourteen-year-old Mortimer Perrin awoke in his family's small apartment on Division Avenue. The summer of 1902 had just begun, and while most kids his age were still lost in dreams, Mortimer was already up and getting ready for his job. His family had recently moved from New York, and he wanted to help with the household finances. When a friendly dentist hired him to clean,

Mortimer felt like he had struck gold. This job was more than a way to earn money; it was a chance to prove himself and support his family during a challenging time.

That morning, Mortimer decided to surprise his boss by cleaning the office windows. He wanted everything to shine when the dentist arrived. With a bucket of soapy water in hand, he made his way to the Kendall Building, a structure that stood out in the neighborhood due to its unique redbrick and sandstone construction. Located by the Veterans Fountain, the Kendall Building was a well-known landmark, adding to its distinctive charm.

As Mortimer climbed to the second floor, where the dentist had his office, he felt a sense of pride and responsibility. He carefully cleaned the inside of the windows first, making sure every pane was spotless. Then, with a mix of bravery and determination, he stepped out onto the ledge to tackle the outside. The first two windows sparkled under his diligent care, but when he reached the third, disaster struck. As he tossed a cup of dirty water, he lost his balance and tumbled down, landing hard on the ground below. His head hurt badly, and he couldn't move. They rushed Mortimer to the hospital and did everything they could to save him. Despite their best efforts, he died that morning, leaving everyone in shock and sorrow.

Years passed, and the block of buildings that included the Kendall became part of a bustling neighborhood filled with shops and people. Although each building stood independently, they were so close together that they appeared as one continuous row. They housed everything from dime stores to insurance offices, even a dance studio! The sad story of Mortimer had long been forgotten, buried under the layers of time and progress.

In 1997, the triangular building on the corner was transformed into the Grand Rapids Children's Museum, a place filled with laughter and fun. Perhaps it was this joyful atmosphere that drew the spirit of Mortimer back from the beyond. Many visitors have reported feeling a curious energy that lingers in the air, as if someone is watching over them, adding an extra layer of mystery to the museum's charm.

One employee named Evelyn has seen and heard Mortimer's playful spirit. "I see movement out of the corner of my eye," she explained with a smile. "It's like a little kid running around, having fun!" Many times, Evelyn has heard giggles and footsteps when the museum was closed. When it happens, she imagines Mortimer's spirit darting between the exhibits, laughing and playing exactly like the children who visit the museum every day.

Another worker, a teenager

named Jack, had his own spooky experience. While working in the gift shop on a snowy Saturday, he noticed a strange light floating above the bookshelves by the front window. It was a round white ball of light, about the size of a softball. It hovered for a moment before zipping through one of the books that sat on a stand. Then the book flipped forward and the light disappeared. Jack tried to rationally explain what he saw, but before he could come up with anything, a book next to it did the same thing, then the next. In total, five books defied gravity and flipped forward. Jack felt a mix of surprise and wonder. "It seemed like the spirit was just being silly," he said. "I didn't feel scared at all!"

Even more mysterious happenings occur in the basement. Because of the way the buildings are lined up next to each other, they have doors for plumbers and electricians to use to get from one basement to the next easily. But to open the doors, both sides need to unlock their locks. This makes it hard to explain when the store next to the Grand Rapids Children's Museum ends up with balls and blocks on their side, and shoes from their store end up on the museum's side. The mysterious exchanges between the basements add to the eerie yet fascinating aura of the place.

Perhaps the most intriguing story was told by a woman named Julie. She had brought her two nephews to the museum where they were bouncing from one exhibit to another. When they moved downstairs by the yellow car, Julie sat next to a lady there with her son. He was talking to what appeared to be his invisible friend. With a nervous giggle, the mother said, "That's Julius and his amazing imagination!" She went on to say that they came to the museum at least once a week, and her son had recently started talking to a pretend friend—not only at the museum but also at home. "I've been trying to get him out of the house more. He loves watching TV. I think he named his imaginary friend after a character in the Mickey Mouse Clubhouse—Mortimer." Imagine Julie's surprise when, years later, she learned about the sad story that took place one hundred years before, just feet from where she had been sitting.

So, if you ever visit the Grand Rapids Children's Museum, keep your eyes peeled! You might catch a glimpse of Mortimer, the friendly ghost, playing with the children. With all the fun activities, from train tables to LEGOs, it's the perfect place for a child's ghost to spend eternity. Who knows? Maybe Mortimer is still helping kids have the best time ever now that he doesn't have to be up for work the next morning!

Abram W. Pike House

CHAPTER 8

The Ghost of Abram Pike

Port Sheldon, a city in Michigan, started with big dreams. In the 1830s, some investors saw the untouched land and thought it could become a bustling city like Chicago. Located west of Grand Rapids, they built everything a town would need: homes, a post office, a store, and even a railroad. The most amazing building was the Ottawa House hotel, which had twenty-nine rooms and cost $40,000 to build. That was a lot of money back then! The hotel had four huge Greek pillars in the front that made it look stately, like the White House.

But Port Sheldon faced many problems, like a shallow waterway that made shipping impossible. By 1844, the town was abandoned. The investors began to look for someone they could rely on to help them sell off the company's assets. When word got out that they were looking for a dependable man, many suggested they talk to a fellow named Abram Pike.

Abram was an amazing guy! Born on a farm in Ohio, he was known for his hunting skills. He moved to Michigan at thirteen to work at an Indian Mission school, where he learned Native languages and customs. By sixteen, he spoke several dialects and was able to help the local tribes communicate and barter. He loved animals, especially a white pony that went with him on many of his adventures.

Abram was known for his bravery and often helped travelers navigate the rugged terrain of West Michigan. One of his most famous adventures took place during the winter of 1842, a season so harsh it became known as "the hard winter." Temperatures plummeted to twenty-two degrees below zero Fahrenheit, and by mid-November, snow had piled up over two feet deep. This snow remained for five months, making travel extremely difficult. During this time, a ship sailing on Lake Michigan was caught in a terrible snowstorm and wrecked near the shores of Grand Haven. The ship's crew were cold, exhausted, and

wearing clothes that had turned to ice. They needed to find their way to Grand Rapids to catch a stagecoach home to Ohio.

Most guides were too scared to help, but not Abram. He led them on the thirty-four-mile journey through the deep snow and freezing temperatures. The trip was hard; the snow was so deep that the men had to take turns leading the group, throwing themselves into the snow to make a path while the others walked single file behind. Abram's favorite pony, white as the snow, followed at the back, carrying supplies.

By the end of the second day, many of the sailors wanted to turn back, but Abram knew they wouldn't survive if they did. He convinced them to keep going. On the morning of the third day, they met two farmers using oxen to clear a path through the snow. The rest of the journey went quickly, and the group safely reached their destination. This adventure made Abram famous for being tough and smart. He showed everyone how determined he was, even when things got really, really hard. The investors heard about Abram and knew he was someone they could rely on. They hired him on the spot.

After Abram sold off the town's property, he needed to choose a new place to live. He remembered a Christmas Day when he had visited a lovely area called the Grand River Valley (what we now call Grand Rapids). The natural beauty of the place left a lasting impression on him. He and his family set out and built a new home on what is now known as Fulton Street. Most impressive is that Abram dragged the four massive Greek columns from the Ottawa House hotel by oxcart to use on the front of his new home. He also used smaller columns from the train depot on the side porches. He was upcycling before any of us thought it was cool!

Abram's majestic home became known as Pike House, and he and his family lived there happily for many years. His pony lived to be well over forty years old, with the last half of its life spent peacefully grazing the estate. In 1906, Abram died at ninety-three years old. His family lived in the home until 1920, when his daughter gave the property to the Grand Rapids Art Gallery after the original gallery burned down in 1919.

Over the years, Pike House had many additions to fit the growing art collection, but it eventually outgrew the property. Different businesses owned it, including furniture and design companies. In 2018, a law firm called Keller & Almassian bought the property. They worked hard to preserve its history. When they were digging for a new parking lot, they found jars, bottles, and two rusted horseshoes that they believed belonged to Abram's white pony. They now display them in their office.

People who work at Pike House often have the feeling that someone is watching over them. A woman named Dee had several encounters with what she believed was a friendly ghost. One time, Dee lost an important folder. She had been filing all day and worried she had accidentally put it in the wrong place. She knew it would take hours to go through all the cabinets to find it. Feeling defeated, she sat down at her empty desk and closed her eyes, tears welling up. When she opened them, the folder was right on her desk! Dee let out a huge sigh of relief and gratefully thanked her special friend. The ghost had found it for her!

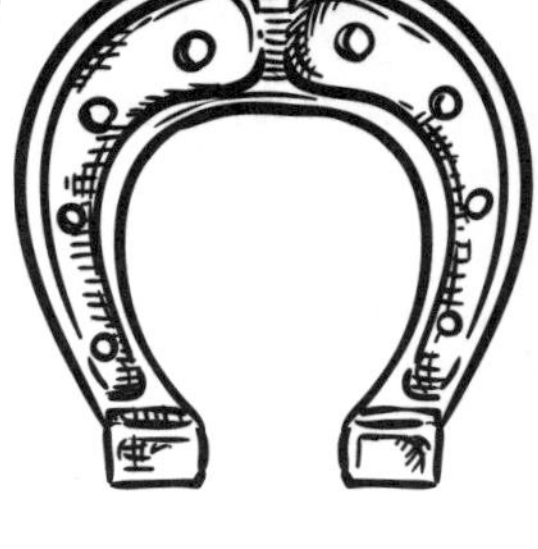

Another time, Dee was walking down the hallway when she saw a man dressed in old-fashioned clothes. He had a beard but no mustache, which she found quite unusual. The man smiled, tipped his hat, and then turned toward the water fountain. To the woman's amazement, he took several steps up what appeared to be an invisible flight of stairs and then vanished into thin air! Dee said she didn't get scared because the ghost was so polite. Later, a picture was found of Abram Pike. In it, he sported a beard with no mustache.

There is only one place in Pike House that some find a bit eerie: a small room toward the front of the home. People have reported hearing men's voices and a man's tired sigh. So why is it creepy? It is rumored that Abram Pike passed away from heart failure in this room. Could it be the death rattle of his last breath they are hearing?

Abram Pike's story doesn't end with his life; many believe his friendly spirit still looks after his old homestead. Pike House is not just a piece of history; it's a place where Abram's presence continues to be felt, watching over the new "family" that has moved in.

CHAPTER

9

The Old Wooden Leg

In the heart of downtown Grand Rapids stands a towering building, constructed in 1926 by the Michigan Bell Telephone Company. Every day, thousands of people pass by, unaware of the eerie history that lies beneath its foundation.

In the early 1900s, a grand old residence stood on the corner of Division Avenue and Fountain Street. This was where Mayor George White and his wife, Sarah, lived. After they passed away, their daughter inherited the property. She married Charles Judd, the inventor of the carpet sweeper. It was then that the place became known as the Judd-White house. Since they already had a beautiful home, they decided to rent it out.

One day, a young couple named Warren and Vashti Rowland moved into the house. They had just gotten married, despite Vashti's parents' concerns. Her parents worried because the couple often argued and both had fiery tempers. Warren worked on the railroad, while Vashti had always dreamed of running a boarding house. When they saw the ad to rent the Judd-White house, they thought everything was falling into place.

Months passed, and the neighbors soon grew weary of the couple's constant bickering. Vashti had a knack for provoking Warren, especially after they had too much to drink. Their arguments often spilled out onto the streets, sometimes becoming physical. Vashti had a habit of hitting Warren on the head when she got upset. On another occasion, Warren was seen chasing Vashti through the alley with a razor, threatening to kill her if he caught her.

One tragic day at work, Warren had a terrible accident. He was hit by a train and lost his leg. Although doctors fitted him with a wooden one, people say Warren became even more insecure and jealous when it came to Vashti.

Because of the couple's constant fighting, boarders never stayed long. Without enough

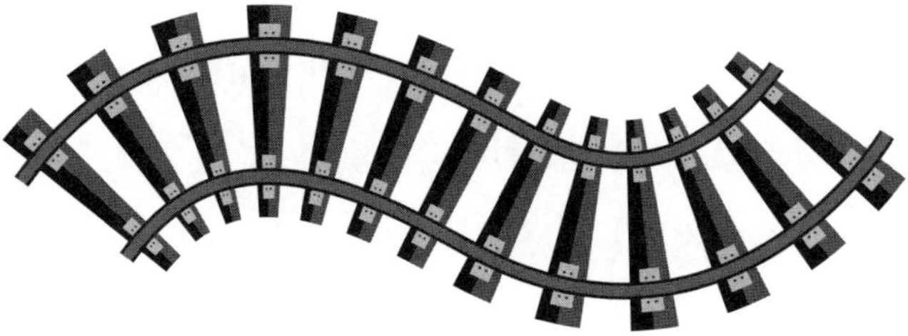

money to pay the rent, they were eventually evicted from the Judd-White house. Finally, they filed for divorce. Vashti told her lawyer that Warren was abusive, while Warren told his lawyer that Vashti drank too much, refused to stay home, and never had his meals ready on time. They went their separate ways.

A couple weeks later, Warren received an unexpected inheritance from a family member. Missing his wife, he went to tell Vashti the good news about the money. Since finances were one of their main issues, Vashti decided to give their marriage one last try.

On June 26, 1907, Warren and Vashti were seen having a great time together. They rented a car and partied all night. At one point, Warren took off his wooden leg to get some money he had hidden inside. He had over $300 shoved inside it! Eventually, it began to rain, so they returned the car and walked off into the night.

The next day, someone went to visit Vashti at her home, but she wasn't there. Both she and Warren had disappeared. Days went by with no word from either of them. Even the police couldn't figure out where they had gone. Then, two weeks later, a neighbor noticed a strong smell of gas coming from the Judd-White house. She called the gas company, and when a worker entered the house, he found a horrifying scene.

Inside, there were two bodies on the bed that looked blackened and burnt, but it wasn't because of a fire. The gas fumes in the room were so strong that they turned the bodies black and even killed the maggots that had gathered on them. If it weren't for the wooden leg, the police would never have been able to identify them.

To this day, no one knows for sure how Vashti died. She may have suffocated from drinking too much, or perhaps she went to sleep and Warren turned on the gas to ensure she never woke up. It was determined that Warren intentionally killed himself. Did he wake up to find Vashti dead and decide he couldn't go on, or did he kill her? Another puzzle is that the money that Warren kept in his wooden leg had completely vanished. This led some people to speculate that maybe it was a robbery made to look like a murder/suicide. The mystery remains unsolved.

Despite the bad reputation the house had gained, a new boarder moved in. People thought he was crazy for living in a house where something so terrible had occurred. He laughed at them—but not for long. Exactly thirteen days later, he was found dead in that exact same bedroom. When they placed his body in a coffin in the front room for the funeral, a breeze came out of nowhere. It tipped a candle over and set the curtains on fire! The flames spread quickly, and soon the whole room was ablaze. By the time the fire was put out, the coffin and the body inside were completely burned.

After that, no one wanted to live in the house. Kids in the neighborhood said they saw strange lights and heard eerie noises coming from the empty building. Some even claimed to see a ghostly woman screaming in the windows. The house became the center of many dares and spooky stories. After the house sat vacant for some time, it was torn down and replaced with the Michigan Bell Building. But the ghosts didn't seem to care about the new owners. People still reported seeing strange things.

A woman named Linda was on the fourth floor one day using the bathroom. While in the stall, she heard someone else go into the stall next to her. The odd thing was that she heard what sounded like a long skirt dragging on the floor. Linda finished her business, came out, and started washing her hands. When she looked in the mirror, she saw what appeared to be old-fashioned woman's boots in the stall behind her. The room had gotten cold, and she felt extremely uncomfortable. As she turned off the water, she looked up into the mirror and saw a woman standing directly behind her. The woman had dark features but looked gaunt with dark circles under her eyes. She wore a long dress with her dark brown hair in a bun. Scared, Linda quickly turned around—but no one was there. She shrieked and ran back to her desk, where there were other people. She was relieved when she was transferred to a new office two weeks later. This same ghost had been seen by others, too.

Security has also had its share of issues in the building. To gain access, workers must scan a card that identifies them to security. However, security is frequently called to check the building in the middle of the night because alarms go off when doors open without any scans.

In recent years, people in Grand Rapids started getting strange phone calls with nothing but static or silence. When the calls were traced, they came from the second floor of the Michigan Bell Building, even when it was closed. Could it be the ghosts trying to reach out for help? No one knows for sure, but it seems the old house's ghosts are still around, haunting the new building. Some nights, if you listen closely, you might hear the faint sound of a wooden leg tapping on the floor.

CHAPTER 10

The Ada Witch

In the small town of Ada, there's a spooky legend that everyone knows. They call her the Ada Witch, and her story has been told for many years. People say they've seen her ghost, but no one really knows who she was.

Legend has it that a young woman, who was married, had a secret. She was meeting another man in the woods near her home, which is now part of Seidman Park. Her husband started to get suspicious and decided to follow her one night. He saw her with the other man and got very angry. In his fury, he confronted them, and a terrible fight broke out.

The husband ended up killing his wife. Then, he turned his rage on her lover, attacking him with a hunting knife. In the scuffle, both men were badly hurt. They all died in the woods that night.

Many people have tried to find historical evidence that this legend is true, including historians and journalists. To this day, no one has been able to prove this event ever took place. Over the years, people have reported seeing her ghost, often described as a woman wearing a long, flowing blue dress, wandering the area and pleading for help. The eerie nature of these sightings and the tragic backstory contributed to her being called the "Ada Witch," even though there's no evidence that she was an actual witch.

In 2003, a group of amateur ghost hunters announced that they had figured out who the Ada Witch was. Based on the supposed age of the woman who was killed and then buried in the cemetery, they concluded that her name was Sarah McMillan. This spread quickly, especially among the local teenagers looking for an adrenaline rush. They would dare each other to visit Sarah's grave at midnight with nothing but a lit candle and a mirror to try to summon Sarah's spirit by saying her name three times. The dare was to stay calm and not run away, no matter what spooky sounds or shadows they might see.

Ada Township was not happy about all this. Not only was it disrespectful to the dead, but the thrill seekers were trespassing and littering. One person, who obviously didn't worry about karma, even started selling pieces of Sarah's tombstone online. "You too can have a piece of the Ada Witch!" the listing read. It was chiseled away until nothing remained to mark Sarah's burial spot. Police began to patrol the cemetery closely to stop the vandals, but the damage was already done.

A well-known paranormal group, the West Michigan Ghost Hunters Society, saw how Sarah had been disrespected. After countless hours of research, they found that Sarah McMillan was not the Ada Witch. She was a twenty-nine-year-old woman who died in 1870 from a bacterial infection called typhoid. She was laid to rest next to her other family members in Findlay Cemetery.

They contacted several headstone companies and explained the situation. The Lowell Granite Company immediately offered to help. They jumped into action, making a new thick and heavy headstone for Sarah McMillan's resting place. They even went so far as to put that she died of typhoid on the tombstone, hoping that people would realize she was not the Ada Witch and leave her stone alone.

While the legend remains questionable, that doesn't mean that someone or something isn't haunting the area. Over the years, many credible witnesses have come forward to share what they have seen.

One night, a lone driver named Mark was making his way home near the intersection of Honey Creek and 2 Mile Road. The fog was so thick that his headlights barely pierced through it. As he approached the corner to turn, he saw her. She stood in the middle of the road, her blue dress billowing in the wind, her blond locks cascading down her shoulders. Her face was pale, her eyes hollow, and her mouth open in a silent scream.

Mark slammed on the brakes, his heart pounding in his chest. The woman was waving her hands in the air. He hesitated, but something compelled him to step out of the car. As he approached, he could hear her desperately begging for help. The sound was otherworldly, sending shivers down his spine.

As Mark got closer, he felt compelled to reach out to touch her. Despite her looking solid, his hand passed right through her. She let out a blood-curdling scream, and in an instant, she vanished into the fog. Terrified, Mark stumbled back to his car and sped away, the image of her haunting eyes burned into his memory.

Other people have seen the same woman throughout Seidman Park and along Conservation Street. One man named Jake, an avid hunter, was deep in the woods when the sun began to set, casting long shadows through the trees. He noticed the forest was eerily silent. Jake had heard stories of the Ada Witch but dismissed them as folklore.

As he was making his way out of the woods, he heard leaves and sticks cracking, as if someone was walking near him. He caught a flicker of movement out of the corner of his eye. Turning quickly, he saw a flash of blue fabric disappear behind a tree. His curiosity piqued, Jake cautiously approached the spot. The air grew noticeably colder as an unsettling feeling washed over him.

Then, he felt a couple light taps on his shoulder. He froze, too terrified to turn around. Gathering his courage, Jake slowly turned his head. Standing just a few feet away was a woman in a long, flowing blue dress. Her face was ghostly pale, almost translucent, with hollow, sunken eyes that seemed to stare right through him. Her lips were cracked and bloodless, twisted into a sorrowful, haunting expression. Dark shadows framed her eyes, giving her an almost skeletal appearance.

She took a step toward him. In a panic, Jake stumbled backward, tripping over a tree root and falling to the ground. When he looked up, she was gone. The forest was silent once more, but the feeling of being watched lingered. Jake scrambled to his feet and ran back to his truck, the image of the woman forever etched into his mind. He never returned to those woods again, and he purposely avoids driving in the area.

To this day, drivers around Seidman Park report seeing the Ada Witch, her mournful cries echoing through the night. They say if you listen closely, you can hear her wailing for help, forever trapped between this world and the next.

A Ghostly Goodbye

As we wrap up our spooky journey through the haunted history of Grand Rapids, I hope you had fun exploring these eerie tales and mysterious encounters. From haunted houses to ghostly figures, Grand Rapids is a city full of spine-tingling stories that bring its past to life in the most exciting ways.

Whether you believe in ghosts or not, these stories show how history and legends can make a place even more interesting. Each ghostly encounter is like a puzzle piece, helping us better understand the city's rich and sometimes spooky past. Remember, the past is always with us, hiding in the shadows and waiting to be discovered by curious minds like yours.

Thank you for joining me on this ghostly adventure. If you ever visit Grand Rapids, keep an eye out for the spirits that might still be wandering around. And if you want to hear more spooky stories, you know where to find me!

Until next time, stay curious, stay brave, and keep exploring the mysteries of the world around you.

Stay spooky, friends!

By day, **Julie Rathsack** is a business insights manager; by night, she's a history-loving ghost hunter! Her fascination with the paranormal began in childhood, growing up in a haunted house where she could hear and sometimes see spirits.

Julie co-authored her first book, *Ghosts of Grand Rapids*, in 2013 and followed it with *A Haunted History of Grand Rapids* in 2024. Her books blend eerie tales with true history, captivating readers of all ages.

When she's not writing, Julie leads haunted tours with Paranormal Michigan Inc. and serves as president and founder of the Lifted Veil Paranormal Investigations group. She's explored countless spooky spots, making her the local expert on ghosts.

At home, Julie lives with her high school sweetheart, their two sons—David and Sam—and a lively household of pets, including three cats and a dog named Oreo. She is a storyteller, historian, and loving mom, making her a true ghost hunter extraordinaire!

Check out some of the other *Spooky America* titles available now!

Spooky America was adapted from the creeptastic *Haunted America* series for adults. *Haunted America* explores historical haunts in cities and regions across America. Here's more from the original *A Haunted History of Grand Rapids* author, Julie Rathsack: